23 SHOCKINGLY SIMPLE
SALES IDEAS

23 SHOCKINGLY SIMPLE SALES IDEAS

For Sellers, Start-ups, and Small Businesses

Make Money, Boost Motivation, Improve Sales Training, and Make Sales Easy and Fun Again

Chris Lytle

www.InstantSalesTraining.com
ISBN-13: 9780692914380
ISBN-10: 0692914382
Library of Congress Control Number: 2017954118
Instant Sales Training, Chicago, IL

Also by Chris Lytle

*The Accidental Salesperson: How to Take Control of Your Career
and Earn the Respect and Income You Deserve*
2nd Edition, AMACOM, 2012

*The Accidental Sales Manager: How to Take Control and Lead Your
Team to Record Profits*
Wiley, 2011

To salespeople everywhere who want to
keep getting better at what they do

Because your clients get better as you get better.

Foreword
by Garfield Ogilvie

My college professors pointed me toward a career in sales. They thought my gift of gab, ability to think on my feet, and boundless enthusiasm would propel me to success. Alas, my innate skills were not enough. Shortly into my sales first job, I was second-guessing my career choice.

It was 1980, and I was selling advertising for the OZFM Network in Saint John's, Newfoundland, Canada. Still I persisted.

I moved to Ottawa and CJSB Radio, an upstart AM station in Canada's capital. There I became a top-ranked salesperson at a bottom-rated radio station.

Things weren't much better. My annual income bordered on what I could make at a minimum-wage job. Then my first child, Mitchell, was born in 1983. I really needed to earn more money.

But I muddled along for a couple of more years, frustrated and disappointed with my lack of success, until I stumbled across an ad in a trade magazine. It was for a seminar called "How to Overcome the Five Toughest Challenges of Radio Sales." The seminar leader was Chris Lytle. I'd never heard of him. Chris was holding the seminar in Buffalo, New York, a five-hour road trip from Ottawa.

I took a chance and signed up for the training. I ponied up the $139 (USD, no less) seminar fee. I hopped in my 1980 Mercury Monarch and drove across Ontario and over the Peace Bridge into Buffalo.

And I met Chris Lytle for the first time. As I listened to his message that day, the fog lifted. I gained new clarity about my sales job.

Chris told us that we should focus on helping our clients sell more rather than focus on selling them more. I learned that, if I could help my client succeed, then my success would follow. This was a fundamental game-changer for me.

Before the seminar, my focus was on how much commission I could make. Afterward my emphasis was on how much I could contribute to the business I was calling on.

That intervention five years into my sales career saved it. Sales were too hard when I saw myself as having to pickpocket my clients to earn a commission. It got easier when I started trying to improve their businesses. I did more homework. I shared my knowledge of marketing and advertising. I focused on their results.

I practiced what Chris preached. For the first time, I felt fulfilled and successful. My income doubled. Soon I was being recruited as a sales manager to show aspiring salespeople how I was succeeding.

A stint as an executive in a national trade association followed. I went on to build and lead sales teams in the outdoor advertising space in Toronto, Minneapolis-Saint Paul, Dallas-Fort Worth, and Las Vegas. And I rose to the national VP of sales role for Clear Channel Airports based in Chicago.

But I still remember shuffling down to Buffalo thirty-two years ago to hear Chris Lytle. It was a smart move. The seminar was six hours long, and I hung on every word. You can read this book in an hour. It's packed with ideas. Chris has the unique ability to simplify every aspect of the sales process.

If these ideas help you, then please let Chris know. He still cares about helping salespeople succeed beyond their wildest dreams.

Garfield Ogilvie is the director of sales and marketing for the PGA Tour's TPC Summerlin, Las Vegas, Nevada (2,612 miles from Saint John's, Newfoundland, Canada).

Author's Introduction

If you love good sales ideas, then you bought the right book. Each chapter contains an idea that will take you a couple of minutes to read and grasp. Each idea is already proven. I've shared them with my seminar audiences, and they've had success with them. Thousands more salespeople get a fresh idea every week from my Instant Sales Training website.

Who am I? Chris Lytle here. You probably know I wrote *The Accidental Salesperson*. I've also been fortunate to travel the world doing sales training. I've reached hundreds of thousands of salespeople on three continents with my programs.

I still hear from many of them. They credit my career-building advice to their success in sales; however, I'm the messenger. They applied the strategies and got better. I hope that happens for you.

There's no theory here, only actionable sales principles.

My advice: Read a chapter when you wake up. Read a chapter when you're in the lobby, waiting for that big meeting. Read a chapter before you go to bed.

Read them more than once, and these ideas will stick with you. Apply them to make an even more powerful impression on your prospects and customers. Of course, you'll make more money too.

Oh, and one more thing. Please share your success stories with me at Chris.Lytle@InstantSalesTraining.com. I'd love to know how you are applying what you learn.

And I'll be shocked if what you're going to take away from this book doesn't make you even more successful. Let's knock this out.

1

Getting Fired for This Was the Best Thing That Ever Happened to Me

It's 1974. I am a twenty-four-year-old know-it-all selling radio advertising in Madison, Wisconsin. On this particular Tuesday, I am meeting with Len Mattioli, the owner of American TV and Furniture.

We are sitting at a dinette set in the furniture department. Len's employees keep interrupting the meeting. When they aren't intruding, Len loses focus on the meeting to make sure customers are getting waited on and sold properly. He can't stay focused on the task at hand, getting the copy ready for the big weekend ad blitz.

When I get back from the meeting, I go into the office of my sales manager, Phil Fisher. "I hate calling on that (bleep) Mattioli," I tell him.

"We don't talk about our customers like that in this company, Chris."

"But he wasted an hour of my time," I shoot back.

"That's your problem. You're fired. Go home and think about what Len's problems are. If you come back tomorrow and you've figured that out, I'll hire you back."

I go home with another problem, the potential loss of my job. But instead of worrying about being fired, I start thinking about Len's problem. The next morning I am at American TV and Furniture at ten o'clock when it opens.

"Len, you've got a problem," I say.

"What's that?" he wonders.

"You spend an hour or two with me to get a couple of sixty-second spots written. Then you meet with all the other reps and do the same thing. You've got to be spending twelve hours getting copy done. Why don't you let me handle all your production? I'll even meet you after hours when you can focus on advertising alone. That way you can get a week's worth of advertising done in an hour. That gives you eleven hours back to work on all the other things you have to get done."

"How much would you charge me?" he asks.

I think for a minute and ask, "Why don't you pay me a thousand dollars a month in merchandise?"

"Deal," he says.

"Thanks, Len. I need some new bedroom furniture."

I got my sales job back and picked up a second job where I handled the advertising for one of the biggest accounts in the market.

It happened when I took the best sales advice anyone has ever given me: "Quit worrying about your problems and start worrying about your customers' problems."

Thanks, Phil.

2

Is It This Easy to Succeed?

Years ago I jumped into an elevator in a San Francisco hotel, and I was face-to-face with Brian Tracy, the famous speaker and prolific author of books on sales and business success. He was on his way down to conduct a seminar for at least fifteen hundred attendees. I was on my way to conduct a seminar for forty-three people.

Years later I jumped onto YouTube and typed "wealthy" into the search bar. A Brian Tracy video popped up. I watched "5 Reasons Why Most Don't Become Wealthy." You should too.

Here's the nugget in case you don't have time right now: "The primary cause for underachievement and failure is that the great majority of people don't decide to be successful."

Now, each chapter in this book offers ideas that will help you sell better. But if you haven't decided you want to sell better, you may not act on these ideas. So decide already. Decide you're going to be successful. Do it now. Otherwise you'll underachieve.

All the good things that happened in my career occurred after I decided I wanted to do something to

- become a top salesperson,
- start my own business,
- write *The Accidental Salesperson,*
- write *The Accidental Sales Manager,*
- create an online course,
- build InstantSalesTraining.com to share hundreds of great sales ideas,
- write this book, and
- help my wife, Sarah, start another business in a whole new industry.

Here's the definition from *Merriam-Webster*'s Online Dictionary:

decide, verb
> a: to make a final choice or judgment about <decide what to do>
> b: to select as a course of action—used with an infinitive <decided to go>

You have to *decide* to be an excellent salesperson. You have to *decide* to become an industry expert. You have to *decide* to become a source of business advantage to your customers.

So have you decided that you want to have a million dollars (or more) in investments, savings, and property? Or hasn't it occurred to you that you can make that decision?

You can decide right now. Once you've decided, every one of the ideas in this book will be even more valuable to you.

3

Unclog Your Sales Pipeline with These Two Ideas

Is your sales pipeline clogged with dead and dying deals? Maybe it's because you're hooked on "hopium."

You *hope* you're going to make the sale. You tell the sales manager you have a hot prospect and you *think* you're going to close the deal. Then nothing happens.

The process of getting hooked starts when a prospect says, "I'm interested; call me next week." You dutifully make a note to call next week. Then you leave.

And guess what? When you call next week, that interested prospect doesn't pick up the phone or answer your emails.

A leading indicator of sales success is the number of prospects who have you on their calendars for a next step. "Interested" prospects don't buy; "engaged" prospects do.

Use the "magic question" the next time a prospect feigns interest and asks you to call next week. You'll inquire, "Are you willing to work with me on a calendar basis?"

Real prospects put you on their calendars for a next step. They engage. Information seekers will blow the smoke of "hopium" your way to politely get rid of you. They play hide-and-seek rather than play it straight.

Never put information seekers into your company's sales projections. You can't afford to have your chief financial officer hooked on "hopium" either.

Next, use the magic email to get stalled deals moving. When a prospect quit returning my phone calls and emails, I sent him this email:

Subj. Quick Question

Cliff,

I have you on my "waiting for" list of people I'm expecting to hear back from. Am I still on your radar?

Chris

He got back to me in two minutes. The deal closed later in the week.

Salespeople on three continents swear by this two-sentence email. Why it works: "Quick Question" is the best subject line I've ever tested. Plus, prospects respect the fact you're persisting professionally. Use the magic email today to get stalled deals moving through and dead deals out of your pipeline and your company's projections.

4

Seven Awesome Ways to Use the Chart

Want to take your sales career to the next level? Great! To do that, you need to know what level you've already attained and what the next level you want to achieve looks like. Evaluating your sales behavior and your current relationships using the Chart will help.

My premise is that the quality of every meeting is measurable. Your meeting objective is measurable on a one-to-four scale. You can measure your pre-meeting preparation on the same scale. And so on.

I always give my audiences time to read and think about the Chart. I want you to do the same. As you read through the Chart for the first time, see if you can visualize yourself at different levels with different prospects and customers.

See how easy it is to measure the quality of the last meeting you had. By the way, the last meeting is the relationship.

11

The Chart

	❶	❷	❸	❹
Objective ▶ To open doors; to "see what's going on"	To persuade and make a sale or to advance the prospect through the process	Customer creation and retention; to "find the fit" to upgrade the client and gain more information	To continue upgrading and increase share of business	
Level of Trust ▶ Neutral or distrustful	Some credibility	Credible to highly credible; based on salesperson's history	Complete trust based on established relationships and past performance	
Approach & Involvement ▶ Minimal or non-existent	Well-planned; work to get prospect to buy into the process	True source of Industry Information and "business intelligence"	Less formal and more comfortable because of trust and history	
Concern or Self-Esteem Issues ▶ Being liked	Being of service, solving a problem	Being a resource	Being an "outside-insider"	
Pre-Meeting Preperation ▶ Memorize a canned pitch or "wing it"	Set objectives; pre-script questions; articulate: •purpose •process •payoff	Research trade magazines, Internet; analyze client's competition	Thorough preparation, sometimes with proprietary information unavailable to other reps	
Point of Contact ▶ Buyer or purchasing agent	Owner, end users as well as buyer or purchasing agent	C-Level, end users and an "internal coach" or advocate within the client's company	"Networked" through the company, may be doing business in multiple divisions	
Presentation ▶ Product literature, spec sheets, rate sheets	Product / service solution for problem uncovered during needs analysis	Systems solutions	ROI proof and profit improvement strategies	

In my live presentations, I'll ask the audience members to come up with things they can *do* with the Chart besides leaving it in their handouts. Here are my seven favorite ideas that came from real salespeople:

1. Use the Chart to grade a meeting you just had and/or the relationship you currently have with the customer.
2. Use the Chart to plan an upcoming meeting with a prospect or customer. See if you can include some level-two, -three, and -four elements or moments in that meeting.
3. Grade each page in your written proposals using the Chart.

    Level 1: The page is about your product, company, or pricing.

    Level 2: The page is about a problem your prospect wants to solve.

    Level 3: The page has information about industry issues or norms.

    Level 4: The page includes information about the customer's customer.

    Grade each page. Add up the scores. Divide by the number of pages. You'll end up with a score for the whole proposal. If it's not level two or higher, it's product focused rather than client focused.

    See how that might be helpful?

4. Put the Chart on the wall and refer to it before you dial the phone or walk out the door. This can remind you to make your approach a higher level one.
5. Take a copy of the Chart to any client who has salespeople. Say, "I found this chart helpful. I thought you might want to use it with your sales team." Chances are the client will start thinking of you as a resource. Wow, you've just had a level-three moment that differentiates you from the competition.
6. A few brave salespeople suggest you share the Chart with a client and ask him or her to grade you. How are you doing? What could you do to improve?
7. Ask a customer to read the Chart and then tell you what kind of relationship he or she wants with you. A salesperson told me his story about doing this and said it improved the relationship within a few weeks.

Are you going to act on one or two of the seven ideas? Your clients get better as you get better. And your clients are rooting for you to get better. What client doesn't want to work with higher level salespeople?

If you really want to take your sales career to the next level, then follow the Chart.

5

The Shockingly Simple Closing Technique

Every salesperson should dread hearing, "Send me a proposal." These four words can add hours of work to your day, not to mention days and weeks to your sales cycle.

Look, not every sale is an enterprise solution. Not every product is customizable. Sometimes we're just out there selling stuff that solves a common business problem.

Quick story: It's 2004. I'm a fifty-four-year-old sales trainer. I'm in South Bend, Indiana, meeting with the chief financial officer (CFO) of a broadcast company.

We're ninety minutes into the first meeting. He's hesitant to invest in sales training. His sales managers are having trouble finding good candidates to train. There is too much turnover.

I also happen to sell an aptitude test for evaluating potential employees. I steer the conversation toward selecting better salespeople.

"This is exactly what we need," says the CFO. "Send me a proposal for fifteen of them."

The tests cost one hundred dollars each. "I brought an order form," I reply.

There's silence. "That will work," says the CFO.

It's a done deal.

"I brought an order form" is the shockingly simple close that will work for you. It will save you a lot of work writing proposals.

Sometimes you have to simplify the sales process for the buyer and yourself. By having an order form at the ready, I put the deal in writing without having to do hours of customization. Nor did I have to drive 150 more miles to have the second meeting.

"I brought an order form" is a shockingly simple close because if the prospect really wants to buy, there's nothing else you need to say.

6

Window Shopping

Sarah and I are in Brevard, North Carolina, in the spring of 2013. It is the next to last day of our vacation. Earlier in the vacation, we had visited Thomas Jefferson's Monticello in Charlottesville, Virginia. Then we drove to Asheville, North Carolina, specifically to see the Biltmore Estate. Both were on Sarah's bucket list of architectural wonders to see and well worth the trip.

If you want to see how beautiful this area is, catch *The Hunger Games*. Several scenes were shot in the Dupont State Recreational Forest.

So now we're just driving around looking at waterfalls and visiting little towns in the Asheville area, which is how we happen to be window shopping on Brevard's Main Street.

Sarah and I are walking past an art gallery. I look around, and she is stopped dead, looking and laughing at something in the window. "Come and look at this," she says. "*This* is a life-size statue of a white squirrel."

Brevard County is famous for its white squirrels, and local artists apparently make a good living depicting them. And in this particular depiction, the white squirrel is standing upright, holding an acorn like a football in one paw. The other paw is extended like a football running back, straight-arming an opposing defender. Think Heisman Trophy with a squirrel instead of a human. So we're standing there, deciding if we like the squirrel enough to buy it.

Suzie is working the counter inside and sees us looking in the window. She comes to the front of the gallery and opens the door. "You don't have to press your noses against the window to see what's inside. Come in. Look around and be comfortable," she says.

When we walk in, she tells us two quick stories:

1. "This gallery carries only works of local artists from Transylvania County. I'm one of them."
2. "Each one of us works here a couple of days a month to keep the place going."

Sarah and I look around and finally decide against the squirrel. As we walk toward the door, we pass a jewelry counter with, again, locally made stuff.

I see a striking pendant in the case. I point at it, and Suzie takes it out and hands it to Sarah.

When we turn it over, the price is a couple of hundred dollars *less* than what I would have been willing to pay. I quickly whip out my Visa card to buy it. Suzie hands me the receipt, and we're on our way.

As I reflect on our experience, I am reminded of the book *What Great Salespeople Do.* Michael Bosworth and Ben Zoldan write about the importance of having a company story and a "why I'm here" story.

Suzie managed to tell me those two stories in thirty seconds or less. "This gallery only has the work of local artists from Transylvania County, and each of us works here a couple of days a month. Today is my day."

And I'm glad it was her day.

The football-playing squirrel stopped Sarah in her tracks. In business-to-business sales, your white squirrel could be a startling statement, a statistic, or a story about a successful customer. "We just helped Client A realize a twenty-three percent savings." Or "We just helped Client A gain twenty-three new clients."

Suzie's two stories encouraged us to look around and buy.

I look for sales lessons even when I'm on vacation because I know I'll need them for a book like this or for my website. Do you look for lessons by paying attention to how well salespeople sell to you? And then do you apply them to you own sales job?

Watch out for good ideas and football-playing squirrels.

Two Questions to Help You Win Back Lost Customers

You screwed up big time. Or the salesperson before you screwed up. (It doesn't matter what it was or how it happened.) The customer got upset and canceled an order or quit doing business with you altogether. It happens. But time passes. People leave; people forget. What does that mean to you?

It means your best prospecting tool is that list of former customers. Find out the reason they quit doing business with you and what you need to do to fix it. They've bought already. They wanted to do business with your company at one point.

All you have to do is call them up and say, "I would like to win back your business and have you as a customer again. What would have to happen for that to occur?"

Some will appreciate your concern. But not everyone will be glad to hear from you. The former client may still be mad. Not mad at you necessarily, but at whatever happened.

Let the former client vent. Listen with empathy. Agree with his or her right to be righteously angry. Then ask, "What is the statute of limitations on that offense?"

Don't ask this in a flippant way. Ask in a soft, calm, nonthreatening, curious voice, "What is the statute of limitations on that offense?"

Look, you didn't kill anyone. Nobody should receive a life sentence for a business misdemeanor.

What are you waiting for? Start working that list of former customers. How about starting with three to five names. Call each. Have a conversation.

Now you have the best way to start the conversation. "I would like to win back your business. What would have to happen for that to occur?"

The customer may tell you what to do, and you can comply. Or the customer may still be angry, and you can use the second question, "What is the statute of limitations on that offense?"

Now what would have to happen for you to use this idea this week? Today?

If you're enjoying this book, then you're going to love my website.

Want more of these sales stories and ideas? Who wouldn't?

You're reading a compilation of the scripts I've used for my Instant Sales Training audio MP3 posts. My loyal subscribers have been implementing these ideas for the past two years.

Here's what they're saying about it:

Resonates with my team and their reality

> I look forward to sharing the weekly knowledge bite with my team. It creates a useful discussion within my sales organization.

> —Iain Pound, national sales director, Racquet Sports, Wilson Sporting Goods

Comprehensive and helpful

It's like having my own sales guru on call. I can find a solution to a sales problem. I can get a quick idea to move sales forward. Or I can download a motivational thought to share with a salesperson who needs one.

—JOE KOFF, VP OF TRAINING AND DEVELOPMENT AND CHIEF OPERATING OFFICER, RING OF HONOR WRESTLING

Usable sales ideas and best practices

Chris has been my go-to for any sales issue or bump in the road. This is a logical extension of delivering his content. Even my veteran salespeople find new ways to utilize the techniques and information.

—TOM ENGLISH, CHIEF REVENUE OFFICER, CROMWELL, NASHVILLE, TENNESSEE

Imagine getting a fresh sales idea each week. Plus you gain instant access to the archive of more than one hundred Instant Sales Training MP3s.

You can download them in seconds and listen to them on your device on the way to see a client.

Hey, even when I was doing six-hour seminars, most people were happy to leave with one good idea. Now you can get a good idea in minutes and implement it right away.

Who's got time to go to marathon training sessions anymore? These users like the content and the time savings:

Concise and targeted

> *Look, too many salespeople have the attention span of a four-year-old on Kool-Aid. Fast-moving sales meetings translate to pumped-up reps. And it's made me a better trainer and a more effective manager.*
>
> —CRAIG WHETSTINE, VP/GENERAL MANAGER, WERL/WRJO

Keeps us growing

> *Every week, I find the topic extremely relevant to our improvement. When our sales team gathers to discuss the knowledge bite, there's never a shortage of stories about how they are applying the material in the field.*
>
> —KEVIN M. KELLY, VP OF SALES AND STRATEGIC INITIATIVES, INDIANA FARMERS MUTUAL INSURANCE, INDIANAPOLIS, INDIANA

Get a little bit better every day instead of trying to do it all at once. Now, typically I charge $143 for a one-year subscription to Instant Sales Training.

But because you've bought my book, and because you're going to tell five friends and colleagues about it, and because I really want to help you, you can buy a single subscription for a full year at a serious discount if you visit my website, www.InstantSalesTraining.com. (This is a limited-time offer for readers only.) Use the promo code SHOCK at checkout to get the deal (not case sensitive).

Relevant and timely

Instant Sales Training is just-in-time learning that affords a sales manager a consistent way to keep their team pursuing continuous improvement.

—JOHN DAVIS, HIGH GEAR TRAINING AND HIRING SYSTEMS, BALTIMORE, MARYLAND

Engaging, provocative, inspiring, and actionable

My team loves your Instant Sales Training sessions. They are an integral part of our weekly sales meetings.

—LEO BAGGIO, GENERAL MANAGER, JIM PATTISON GROUP, CRANBROOK, BRITISH COLUMBIA, CANADA

Go to www.InstantSalesTraining.com to learn more about Instant Sales Training. Use the promo code **SHOCK** at checkout (not case sensitive). Get a full year of shockingly simple sales ideas.

Right here. Right now.

8

Free Sales Seminar on the Bourbon Trail

The Cromwell Radio Group's Bud Walters is a longtime friend and client. He books me to do some management training. My wife, Sarah, and I drive to Nashville for the presentation. On the way back to Chicago, we get some great sales training.

That's because we decide to mosey on back to Chicago through Kentucky. We want to check out the Bourbon Trail. We check into the lovely and historic Beaumont Inn in Harrodsburg, Kentucky. From there we embark on tours of Woodford Reserve and Buffalo Trace. We also visit Four Roses, Maker's Mark, and the Town Branch Distillery in Lexington, Kentucky.

The Woodford Reserve tour costs ten dollars per person. The Buffalo Trace tour is free. Both last an hour. We learn about the distilling process, the importance of the limestone-filtered spring water in making bourbon, and how the white oak barrels can only be used once to make bourbon. It's a federal law.

The best parts of the tours are the stories. Our guides tell us tales about the founders and of surviving Prohibition. They give us real history lessons. Each tour ends with two very small tastings and then drops us off in a well-stocked gift shop.

Each gift shop sells the bourbon, of course. Funny, it costs the same amount that you would pay at your local liquor store. Then there are some very expensive small-batch bourbons that are never shipped out of Kentucky. You can buy those too.

You can also buy expensive logo glassware, coasters, T-shirts, and hats, and the bourbon-flavored candy is nice. Where's the sales lesson?

Right here. Right now. Getting people on your turf is a great way to build strong relationships. The bourbon makers know that people who tour the distillery will become higher margin consumers.

You can get this same benefit too. Get your clients on your turf, and they will see the investment that went into your facility. They'll meet some of the good people who work so hard to deliver the product or service you're selling. Most importantly, they'll hear the stories that humanize instead of commoditize your offering.

What are you waiting for? If you want to increase margins, then sell them on a tour of your facility first.

Coming to Chicago? Please ask for a tour of Instant Sales Training's state-of-the-art facility. Or tour the Instant Sales Training site right now.

www.InstantSalesTraining.com

9

The Best Visual Aid

The best visual aid is a blank sheet of paper. I forget who taught me that, but it's still true. Mike Weinberg puts it this way in *New Sales Simplified*: "Bring a pad and pen. Leave the projector at home." Especially for the first meeting.

I like to bring a legal pad in a leather or leatherlike cover and a decent-looking pen. It doesn't have to be terribly expensive, but a nice pen is part of your uniform. It communicates that you're serious about listening, taking notes, and making the meeting about the prospect, not your product. Too many salespeople want to bring in the product literature. Resist that impulse.

As a sales manager, I remember introducing a new program or product. The first thing salespeople would ask is, "Can we get a one-sheet on that?"

Passing out product literature is a level-one behavior, according to the Chart.

Of course you can bring a one-sheet. But the more one-sheets you have, the more you tend to pass them out. And too many salespeople pass them out way too early. And "way too early" means any of the following things:

- before you've established a problem or opportunity your product addresses
- before you've had a longer conversation about that problem or opportunity
- before you've established your own credibility by telling a story of a business you've helped

Product literature is fine, but it is never better than a good story.

And please, when you finally do hand the person across the desk the product literature, let him or her read it. And shut up. I actually meant to say, "Be quiet and let him or her read it."

Resist the temptation to talk while people are reading. They can't read because you're talking. And they can't listen to you very well because they are trying to read. Every time I've been on a ride-along with a salesperson, I've seen this happen.

One more thing, and it's important. Maybe you noticed I mentioned "the person across the desk" from you. Whenever you can, try to sit perpendicular to the prospect rather than across the expanse of a desk. It's symbolic, but you want to be the salesperson who's on his or her side, not an adversary.

Whenever you can get people in a conference room or at a round table, do so. And attempt very hard to hold back your one-sheets until the right time.

"Bring a pen and a pad. Leave the projector at home." That's good advice. Your slide deck isn't as cool as you are anyway.

10

The Phrase That Pays

My friend Derron Steenbergen is the chief revenue officer at Commonwealth Broadcasting. Recently he asked me to critique some YouTube videos of him in action.

He's very good. The production could be better lit, but Derron's content turned on a few light bulbs for me.

"The Six Most Powerful Words in Selling" is my favorite video of his. Here are those six words: "Based on what you've told me." This is the phrase that pays. Derron teaches it to his salespeople and has seen the results. He says it increases closing rates.

It differentiates you from the peddlers who approach prospects with phrases like these:

"Here's what I've got."
"Here's our new package."
"We're having a special on _____ this month."

Approaching the prospect with those opening gambits pegs the salesperson who does so at level one, according to the Chart.

Those opening gambits are weak. You might as well say, "I don't know what you need, but my manager says I need to see more people and sell more of our stuff."

Compare that with this:

"Based on what you told me, here's what I recommend."

Or this:

"Based on what you told me, here's what I put together for you."

The salesperson who starts this way is focusing on solving the problem, not on making a commission. Note: This is a level-two opener, but it's 100 percent better than level one.

If you're not at the point in your sales process where you can say those six words, then you're just pitching. You're peddling. But you're not consulting.

"Based on what you told me" is easy to say, but it's harder to get into a position to say it. That's because it requires more of you.

- *More planning*
- *More preparation*
- *More information gathering upfront*

When that happens you might find yourself building a relationship your competitors can't steal.

If your approach is based on those words, you have to do the work of asking the questions. Your job becomes finding out what pains them and then finding out what outcomes they want.

Make selling about them and what they're trying to accomplish. Not about your quota.

My take? If you want to sell better, then get in position to make your recommendation based on real client needs.

And use the phrase that pays to preface your remarks: "Based on what you told me."

11

Your Customers Want to Hear These Words

I'm sitting in the Northwest Airlines World Perks Club. My flight to England leaves in an hour. I'm not sure how the captain will greet us. I like to hear, "Ladies and gentlemen, we've completed our preflight checklist here in the cockpit. We're now number two for departure. Sit back, relax, and enjoy the flight."

It's reassuring to know that everyone is following procedure. No one knows what goes on behind closed doors unless the person behind the closed doors tells him or her. In this case, it's the pilot.

Of course, it can work in sales too. So what did you do behind the scenes that your prospect or customer didn't see you do? Did you spend three hours working on the presentation? Did you do some pre-meeting research to determine what questions to ask (and not ask)? Did you hold a brainstorming session with your team to customize a solution?

Let your customers know about the work you're doing for them while they're not looking. Let them know you're thinking about them, even though they're not thinking about you.

The captain has a preflight checklist and a script for greeting the passengers. Try using a scripted opening that starts with this magic phrase, "In preparing for this meeting, I..." Then list two or three things you did to prepare. Your customers will appreciate your effort. They will also appreciate you more than they do your competitors.

Why? Because the number one buyer dislike is lack of preparation. Market your preparation before you try to sell your product. You'll have a much more relaxed and receptive customer.

12

This Word Increases Your
Personal Power Immediately

It's our 2016 summer getaway. My wife, Sarah, and I are in the midst of a two-hour drive to a vacation house we're renting in Michigan. Our three cats are along for the ride. We're making great time on I-94 until...

Bang!

We hit a major-league pothole. We watch as the tire pressure indicator drops from thirty-two to twenty-four to four to zero psi in a few seconds. The first thing I say to her is, "Well, this is inconvenient." Because that's all it is. "Inconvenient" is a fine way to describe the things you don't like but aren't disastrous.

We hit a pothole. There was no collision. There are no injuries. We have a flat tire. That's all. It's inconvenient.

I learned to think this way from the late Larry Wilson, the sales and leadership guru. I was watching one of his videos, and he said, "Personal power is having access to and control over the energies and emotions required to optimize and maximize your performance."

Then he told his audience, "Most people never think about what they think about. Have you ever thought about that?"

Here's my takeaway. Too often we think about the event, in this case, the flat tire. Then we think about how we feel. Angry?

But what causes the feeling? Wilson explained it's what we *think* about the event and then what we say about the event to ourselves.

Now, I could have said, "Well, that ruins the first day of our vacation." Or "This is terrible." Or "This shouldn't be happening." But of course it has already happened.

We have a late-model Cadillac ATS. The good news is we can drive another fifty miles on a flat tire. So we drive to a GMC dealership in Benton Harbor and pay $175 for a new tire. It's no big deal.

Thanks, Larry, for teaching me to label things like flat tires, late flights, and canceled appointments as "inconvenient." I believe it has added years to my life. I've learned to think about what I think about. I don't get angry about the small stuff anymore.

What do you say when you talk to yourself?

It's pretty important.

13

No, Dummy, This Market Isn't Different

It's late summer 1972. I apply for my first job after graduation from college. I want to be a newsman at my hometown radio station WCLT-AM and FM in Newark, Ohio.

Bob Pricer, the general manager, offers me a job in sales as he already has two newsmen. I take it!

After a few months on the job, Mr. Pricer calls me into his office and tells me, "Chris, you have real potential. And I want to send you to a training session. I'll pay the five hundred and fifty-dollar fee."

He's sending me to the Radio Advertising Bureau's School for Salesmen. The word "salesperson" wasn't a thing in 1972. He's picking up the tab for the five-day training session. But I have to drive from Newark, Ohio, to New Brunswick, New Jersey.

I go. I learn. And I return.

And when I come to work on Monday morning, one of our senior sellers, Tom, asks, "What did you learn at that seminar?"

"Well, Tom," I say excitedly, "I learned about consultative selling. They said you should ask questions and find out what the client's trying to accomplish. They even gave us a form to help us collect the data. And then I learned a presentation system for selling bigger schedules."

"Chris, all that is great in theory," said Tom unhelpfully. "But this market is different. People around here won't sit still for that amount of time. They're not going to share that kind of information with a salesman."

Tom, an avid chain-smoker, has two ashtrays on his desk. He smokes one Winston cigarette. Then he smokes a Kool. Winston. Kool. All day long.

Since Tom's client list isn't as robust as his smoking habit is, I decide he is not going to be my role model. I ignore his advice and apply the training I am so excited about.

A few weeks later, he stops me in the hall. "I'm hearing a lot of ads for Ron Klein Buick on the air. How did you sell *that* guy?"

"Tom, if I tell you, you won't believe me," is all I say.

You and I get bad and good advice from peers, managers, customers, and sales trainers. I googled "best sales advice you ever got." I found this article, "70 Top Sales Pros Reveal Their Most Impactful Sales Advice Ever."

I'll share my favorite with you now. It comes from Jim Cathcart, author, Hall of Fame speaker, and sales expert. He says,

Doug McDonald, veteran sales manager for Mass Mutual, told me "The goal is not to make a sale. The goal is to make a difference." And if I couldn't make a difference for my customer, then I shouldn't make that sale to him or her. Ever since then, I've seen the value of selling more clearly. That was the beginning of what today I call "relationship selling."

The goal isn't to make a sale. The goal is to make a difference. It's a simple but powerful piece of advice. It can change the way you think and talk about your sales career.

How would you approach your customers differently if your goal were to make a difference? And would you make more sales as a result of that kind of approach?

People can sense when you're truly concerned about their success. They can also tell when you're only focused on yours.

I hope this idea and this whole book make a positive difference for you.

14

Do This to Be More Persuasive

Give off these three vibes:

1. I'm glad to be here.
2. I know what I'm talking about. And...
3. I love what I'm doing.

Here's *Merriam-Webster*'s Online Dictionary's definition of a vibe before I go any further:

vibe, noun
> a characteristic emanation, aura, or spirit that infuses or vitalizes someone or something and that can be instinctively sensed or experienced— often used in plural

What do you want prospects and customers to *instinctively sense* about you when you walk into the room?

Yep, these three things:

1. I'm glad to be here.
2. I know what I'm talking about. And...
3. I love what I'm doing.

When I deliver a live program, I teach the three vibes. Then I'll ask my audience, usually toward the middle or end of the presentation, "Am I giving off those vibes?"

"Yes," they will say in unison.

I ask, "What makes you say that? How can you tell I'm glad to be here?"

"You're smiling," someone will say.

"You use a lot of gestures."

"You move around the room."

"You're not looking at your watch all the time."

I ask, "OK, how do you know that I know what I'm talking about?"

"You quote experts."

"You tell us good stories."

"You make learning fun with discussion and exercises."

"You explain why you're doing the exercise."

I then ask, "OK then, what makes it look like I love what I'm doing?"

"You're having fun. It's obvious."

"You're present."

"You're here for us."

In *Lead the Field*, Earl Nightingale said, "The top 5 percent radiate confidence. They do this by the way they smile, look, and act."

How do you behave when you're glad to be there? How do people know you know what you're talking about? How might a customer sense you love what you're doing? And if you're giving off all three vibes, how do you think your audience of one (or one thousand) might respond to you?

I think they would instinctively sense you're worth engaging with.

15

When the Prospect Says No, You Can Always Say This

Like me, Bob Terson sold advertising for a good living. He's comfortably retired now but still wanted to share his experiences with others, so he wrote *Selling Fearlessly*.

Before he published it, he asked me to critique his manuscript. I read it. I liked it. I made some suggestions. He took some of them. I wrote a recommendation for it that appears at the front of the book.

Bob has a great idea about what to say when the prospect says no. Rather than slink away in defeat, he suggests that you pause and say these words, "It would be a great help if you could tell me why you didn't buy our program."

That's it. Then be quiet and listen while the prospect describes his or her reasons for passing on your offer. If the prospect raises a real objection, then you can address it and ask for the order again.

Terson has found that, when he asks that question and the client can't come up with an answer, he usually closes the sale. This is especially true when the prospect says, "You know, Bob, I really don't know why. I like your program." He would close them on the spot.

I suggest that you put those words on an index card or make them into a screen saver if you don't use index cards. You want to see it every day and to read it out loud until you memorize it.

"It would be a great help if you could tell me why you didn't buy our program."

"Don't give up too early or too easily," says Bob. "I hung in there until I was certain I wasn't going to make the sale. And then I hung in a little bit longer. Napoleon Hill said, 'The interesting thing about a postage stamp is the way it sticks to its job.'"

A little old school? Perhaps. Still, professional persistence can get you the order.

"It would be a great help if you could tell me why you didn't buy my program."

Tweak it. Make it yours.

Persist…professionally…fearlessly. It's your job.

And if you do lose, don't lose the lesson. Find out why.

16

Answering These Questions Will Help You Sell Better Today

What is selling like when you're at your best?

Question 1: How do you *feel* when you're selling at your best?

Question 2: How do you behave? In other words, what would I see and hear if I were watching you on video?

Question 3: How do your customers react to you when you're selling at your best?

If you want to be at your best more often, then it helps to know what selling is like on those days (in those meetings) that you're at your best. Those are the times when you don't need a sales book or a sales trainer to tell you what to do. Those are the times when you're engaged and engaging. Those are the times that make selling such a rewarding career.

Every time I've asked these questions in a seminar, the energy in the room increases palpably. I hope thinking about your answers (or talking about them with another person) increases your energy too.

This book is full of ideas and tips. But I want you to discover what you're already doing well without my help. Describe what selling is like when you're at your very best. When you're selling at your best, you don't need techniques and tips.

To sell at your best more often, all you have to do is recreate those feelings and behaviors that already work for you. Then you can write your own book about selling.

17

Email Subject Lines Get Your Email Read

I've been avoiding a salesperson who keeps calling my cell phone. I guess I asked for it. I left my email and contact information in exchange for the "Special Report: 10 Great Cities to Retire."

A financial services firm is sponsoring the report. I'm not interested in their financial services, though. I just wanted to see the list of cities. Even though I'll be eighty in thirteen years, I'm not about to retire. Plus I've had the same financial investment team in place for forty years and am not looking to jettison that relationship. So I let the new guy's calls go to voice mail.

He still calls every week to ten days. I'm thinking, if he calls one more time, I'm going to pick up, have a conversation, and tell him what I just told you. (He did call back, and I had the conversation.) I rewarded his persistence. Not all clients will, though.

Here's the point: Nobody has to take your call. He or she can ignore you and send you straight to voice mail. Sure, you can leave a compelling voice mail, and you should. Send an email, and it will at least get scanned. And if your subject line is compelling, it will get opened and read.

Remember and heed this advice: The only purpose of the subject line is to get your email opened. Now, it shouldn't be deceptive, but it should induce the prospect or client to open your email and read it.

I've used the subject line "Quick Question" with great success. A website, SubjectLine.com, will help you create compelling subject lines. It's free. And it lets you check the marketability and deliverability of your subject line. They'll ask for your email and let you in.

I gave them my email, and more than a year later, no salesperson has called on me. I do get emails inviting me to their webinars once in a while.

"Quick Question" scores ninety-six out of one hundred on SubjectLine.com. "Winning Idea for Today" scored one hundred points. That's an A+. Using words like "today" and "now" add urgency. And urgency ups your score when it comes to marketability and deliverability. "Just following up" scores eighty-five. That's a C. "Quick tip," "Quick idea," and "And don't look now but..." all score one hundred points.

Get on the site and see if you can score ninety or higher and get more of your emails opened and read.

Your clients get better as you get better. Writing better subject lines is part of doing it better.

"Uh-oh" scores ninety-one points and piques their curiosity. Don't overuse it, though. Check out www.SubjectLine.com. I'm urging you to act and to do something with what you just learned. Education without action is entertainment.

I hope you're enjoying this book. However, I wrote it for your improvement, not your enjoyment.

18

Preparing Your Audience to Buy from You

Sarah and I have season tickets to Chicago's Lookingglass Theatre. One of their offerings is a play called *Bengal Tiger in the Baghdad Zoo*. I know nothing about that play so I read a couple of reviews the day before I attend because I want to know what to expect.

The reviews are decent. *Chicago Sun-Tim*es reviewer Hedy Weiss wrote,

> *The show is about a tiger that haunts the streets of present day Baghdad seeking the meaning of life. When he instinctively bites off the hand of Tom (Walter Owen Briggs), the US Marine who has teasingly tried to feed him, he is immediately shot to death by Tom's fellow Marine, Kev (JJ Phillips). The tiger quickly returns in the form of a ghost in this play in which everyone ends up heavily*

damaged and deeply haunted. Kev, undone by the war, ends up suicidal in a mental hospital. Tom, who survives the tiger's wrath, returns to Baghdad with a prosthetic hand, determined to reclaim the gold-plated pistol and gold-plated toilet seat he looted from Saddam Hussein's palace. These tainted "trophies" will, he believes, assure his financial future.

That review gets me worried about a strange evening at the theater. My next thought is, "How long does this play last?"

See, if I'm going to a strange-sounding play, I want to know how much time I have to invest and how much energy I have to allocate. So I google "Bengal Tiger at the Baghdad Zoo runtime." It's two hours and ten minutes with one intermission. So even if it's terrible, I'll be in bed by 10:15 p.m.

It is not terrible. It is a riveting and thought-provoking production. The Lookingglass Theatre Company has never disappointed in the past. I don't have to read the reviews or worry about the running time. But still I do.

Once I have the basic questions answered, I can do my job as an audience member and enjoy the performance.

What does this have to do with selling? It's simple. Your customer has the same questions about your upcoming performance as I had about the play *Bengal Tiger in the Baghdad Zoo*.

- What's this about? (Purpose)
- What's going to happen? (Process)
- What am I going to get out of this meeting? (Payoff)
- How long is this going to take? (Timing)
- What are your credentials? (Credibility/Story)

Answer those questions before you start the real meeting. You will have a more receptive audience.

19

Sharpen Your Sales Approach by Acknowledging the Obvious

It's a beautiful February weekend in 2017. The temperature has risen to seventy-two degrees. Climate change?

One of Sarah's and my errands is getting our six best knives sharpened at Northwestern Cutlery. The knives are about as dull as our weekend until my royalty check arrives in the mail.

People are still buying *The Accidental Salesperson*. That event caused me to check the top-rated one hundred sales books on Amazon these days. Alas, mine isn't in the top hundred anymore.

I've met the guy who wrote the number-six rated book, *Cold Calling Techniques That Really Work!* Stephen Schiffman's a real character and a really good sales trainer.

Still, I don't order his book. Instead I watch a bunch of his YouTube videos *promoting* the book. Schiffman has a great way to start a conversation with someone who isn't doing business with you.

Schiffman says,

As salespeople, most of the people we try to get a meeting with are people who aren't doing business with us. They're happy with the status quo. One thing you can guarantee from the very first second: You're not my customer. But we don't use that information...We communicate in stories. There's a story about how you got your job. There's a story about why you live where you do. There's a story behind everything we do. So get the story about why the customer isn't buying from us now. If we simply ask the question about what the story is, we get an elaboration. Say, "I know you're not buying from us. I'm just curious why not. I'm curious if you've had meetings with other salespeople from my company." Call it counterintuitive. But use the obvious fact that they're not doing business with you. Get the story of why they're not. Let that [answer] inform some of the next questions you ask and stories you tell.

I like Stephen. I love this idea. I hope you do too.

Sharpen your knives. (It makes them safer.) Sharpen your sales skills. (It will make you money.) Start your phone call or meeting with something you can both agree on. "You're not doing business with us."

Then take it from there. It's worth a stab.

20

The One-Word Answer to Nearly Every Price Objection

I downloaded Art Sobczak's free e-book, *Telephone Tips That Sell: 501 How-to Ideas and Affirmations to Help You Get More Business by Phone.*

I read all 501 of Art's tips, but I keep coming back to this one: "The word 'oh?' can be one of your most powerful questions," he writes.

Art Sobczak should know. His Business by Phone website and training set the industry standard.

"Oh?"

Seriously. Try it.

Art says,

> As salespeople, we think we should answer every objection or defend our company's honor when a prospect says something disparaging about our product, service or the last rep that called on them.

But sometimes you must let people talk. Let them vent.
It will help them clarify their thinking.
So, ask the question, "Oh?"

Add whatever quizzical look you can that shows you're interested in knowing more. (I'm thinking eyes wide open and lips parted.)

Please resist your own tendency to talk and instead ask the other person to talk even more so you can really understand. We know we should listen more.

You shouldn't have to argue your way to sales success. Rather you need to understand your prospects more deeply.

Asking the question "Oh?" and continuing to listen to what your prospect says next will get you closer to that understanding and your next sale.

It communicates you want to listen rather than defend yourself. And it expresses curiosity, a trait too few salespeople exhibit.

Customers buy when they feel understood, not when you make them understand how great your product or service is.

Oh yes, they do.

21

The Three Best Ways to Start a Presentation

As a young professional speaker, I learned about using a startling statement or truism to begin a presentation. A truism is a self-evident, obvious truth. I like this one: "Management is a series of interruptions, which are constantly interrupted by *more* interruptions."

I opened with that when I spoke to a roomful of business owners and managers. I could count on the audience members to sigh and nod in agreement. I used this opening statement on three continents. It worked everywhere because it's a self-evident, obvious truth about management.

Then I would remind my audience that they could invest the next three uninterrupted hours working *on* their business instead of *in* their business. It was an effective opening. It never failed me. It was a great way to get people in the mood to learn.

You too have to get people to engage. They have to be willing to enter a conversation about their business aspirations and issues with you.

Meet Conor Neill, an Irishman who teaches salespeople and executives how to give better presentations. His eight-minute YouTube video is "How to Start a Speech." Of course, you can use any of these ideas to start a sales conversation.

1. If you're at a networking event, you might say, "We may know someone in common." (Of course, you have done your research on LinkedIn before you make that statement.)
2. A shocking factoid is another way to go. "There's more people alive today than have ever died," says Neill. That's one of his shocking factoids. Makes you stop and think, doesn't it?
3. The best way to start a speech is with the words, "Once upon a time..." That signals a story is coming and gets people to lean in.

Stories are always about people, not products and services. They connect us to the people we are calling on in ways that a slide deck or product literature never can.

We all want our prospects and customers to engage with us. The quickest way to have that happen is to be more engaging.

22

Three More Life-Changing Words

When it comes to politics, everybody has an opinion and wants to voice it. We sometimes talk our way out of sales by voicing our opinion too soon.

Sure, we know we're supposed to listen to our customers. But we have our deck, and we've memorized our pitch. And the customer is already rolling his or her eyes and making "hurry up" noises. So we spew.

Dr. Mark Holder has a better idea. He earned his PhD at the University of California at Berkeley. He did his postdoctoral training at the Brain Research Institute at UCLA. There he conducted brain transplants to reverse impairments caused by brain injuries. Now he's an associate professor at the University of British Columbia. He studies and teaches the science of happiness.

The title of his TEDx Kelowna BC talk grabbed me: "Three Words That Will Change Your Life."

Holder takes nearly sixteen minutes to reveal them. So I'll tell them to you right now: "Tell me more."

When you're engaged in a conversation and when you lean forward and look in the person's eyes and simply say, "Tell me more," what it tells the person is that what they're saying is so important, it matters to you so much that you don't want to go on to your story. You don't want to distract them. You don't want to give your two cents worth...I ask my undergraduates why they listen. And they say, "We listen to someone to get information." And they're right. That's a good reason. But if that's the only reason you listen, once you have the information...you stop listening. And you interrupt.

But there's also value to the speaker when we listen... It allows them to express their thoughts and their feelings. It validates the speaker and tells them their story is important. When we listen, it allows the speaker to find solutions just by talking. It allows us to celebrate the success of the speaker. And it allows us to console them if they've had setbacks.

"Tell me more" is a way you can give a speaker all that value by letting that person express more thoughts and feelings.

Without argument or judgment, I might add.

Dr. Mark Holder offers three more words to use to keep the conversation going: "What happened next?" Getting customers to tell you more increases understanding and deepens the relationship.

Watch the whole talk by the former brain surgeon.

Tell me more. What happened next? Has your life changed yet?

Call me when it does: (773) 501–7008.

23

Good Sales Advice? Be Careful What You Google

In closing, I thought you might want another chapter about closing sales. So, to get the ball rolling, I googled "best sales closing lines." What came up were some of the worst closes...ever.

One website lists dozens of old-school, high-pressure manipulative closes. Here's one:

The concession close: "John, if I reduce the price by 10 percent, will you sign the contract today?"

Yikes! That's bad, but not as bad as:

The shame close: "Your son really deserves the new model, don't you think?"

Never mind the **embarrassment** close or the **ask-the-manager** close:

Embarrassment: "This is the cheapest option. This one, however, is the better value."

Ask the manager: "I'm sorry that's all the discount I'm allowed to give. But we're a bit below target and I'm sure if I ask my manager, she might shave a little more off for you. Is that OK?"

In *Spin Selling,* Neil Rackham writes about closing, pressure, and manipulation:

> *In low value sales (given unsophisticated customers and no need to have a continuing relationship) closing techniques can work very effectively. With professional buyers, closing techniques make you less effective. They reduce your chances of getting the business.*

Good advice, Neil.

Look, I'm assuming you don't have a lot of one-call closes. If you do, manipulate away! I'm figuring you're calling on sophisticated buyers who meet with many salespeople.

If I'm right, avoid the closing lines you'll find by googling "best sales closing lines." Like this one:

The level-with-me close: "Polly, level with me. Have I failed to show you the value of what you'll receive from your investment?" (Then be quiet.)

I like the "be quiet" part. But that's it.

That comes from an article for life insurance pros entitled "The 5 Best Closing Lines."

Here's what I wrote in *The Accidental Salesperson: How to Take Control of Your Career and Earn the Respect and Income You Deserve*:

> A Success *magazine survey of a thousand top sales performers found out that more than half had abandoned any kind of closing technique. Some 56 percent of the salespeople said they just looked the client in the eye and said something like, "This is right for you. Let's do it."*

And then they waited for the client to sign the order. I still stand by that advice, especially if you really do believe in what you're selling. If you don't, then this close could come off as phony.

There's plenty of bad sales advice on the Internet. Fear not. I will curate the Internet for you and find ideas that work.

Here's one from thought leader Dave Kurlin:

> Let's assume that you've decided to ask for the order and ask at the right time. When is the right time? It's when you've touched all the bases. You've reached first, second and third and you're sliding into home plate. You haven't taken any shortcuts.

So, what exactly are you asking? You're asking if they want your help. You might have to customize it a little. "Would you like my help closing more sales?" This question is a close anyone can execute. But you still have to ask.

Thanks, Dave. I like it. It's straightforward. It's fresh. And it's devoid of any pressure or manipulation.

Mahan Khalsa, another of my favorite sales thinkers, puts it this way:

Helping clients succeed not only feels better, it is tremendously more effective. It is a powerful, if paradoxical, means of getting what we want.

(I recall Garfield Ogilvie saying almost the same thing in his wonderful foreword to this book.)

And it's also a great reason why "Would you like my help?" will work.

My two cents?

I teach two closes today in seminars and webinars:

1. "I would like to have you as a customer. Is there any reason we can't get started?"

It works because it states what you want. It invites the customer to tell you if there's anything standing in the way of moving forward.

2. "What would you like me to do next?"

It works because it gives the prospect all the control, with no pressure. You just won't find them by googling "best sales closing lines."

Trust me. I've already tried.

Now you know why I'm known for packing more usable information per minute into my books and speaking engagements than any other trainer. Throughout this book, I've mentioned websites and YouTube videos. You can continue your sales education by checking them out. Access the videos I mentioned by going to YouTube and typing the title into the search bar.

The price is right.

Thank you for reading this book. My mission is making successful people successful sooner. I hope, in your case, I've accomplished that mission.

Chris Lytle

September 22, 2017

About the Author

Chris Lytle, best-selling author of *The Accidental Salesperson* and *The Accidental Sales Manager*, was born in Newark, Ohio, and graduated from Baldwin-Wallace College with a political science degree in 1972.

After working as an intern in Congress, Lytle returned to Newark, where he hoped to secure a news position at a local radio station. Instead, he was offered a sales job, which he accepted, changing the course of his career forever.

Lytle started his own business in 1982 and has spent the last thirty-five years delivering domestic and international seminars to salespeople and their managers. He has offered training to Fortune 500 companies and start-ups in the technical, financial, and service industries.

Lytle now lives in Chicago, Illinois, with his business partner and wife, Sarah McCann.

Notes

Notes

Notes

Notes

Notes

Notes

Notes

Notes

Made in the USA
San Bernardino, CA
28 March 2018